AF481070

ALEXANDER THE GREAT

Military Commander and King of Ancient Greece

Biography Best Sellers
Children's Biographies

Speedy Publishing LLC

40 E. Main St. #1156

Newark, DE 19711

www.speedypublishing.com

Copyright 2017

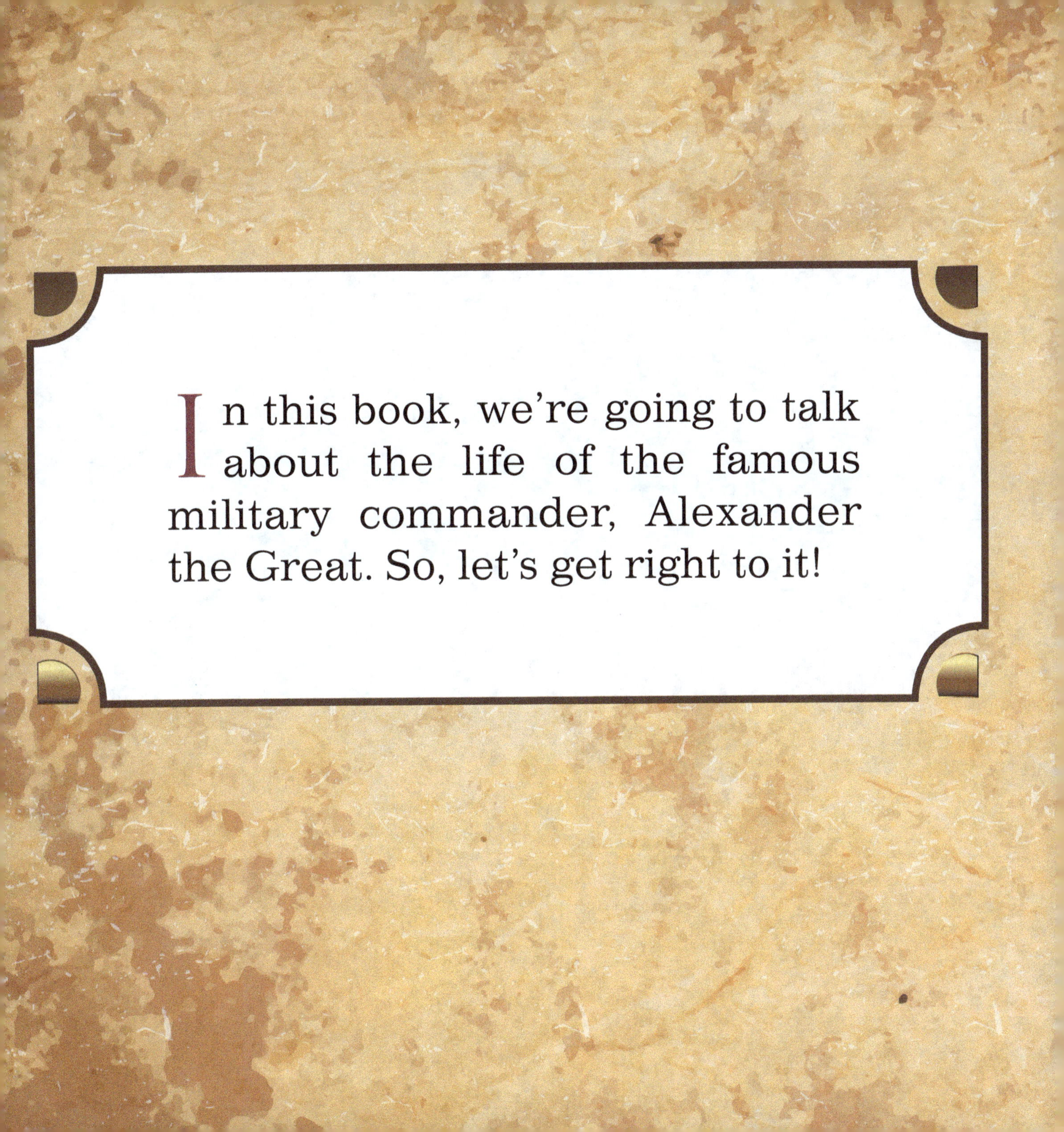

In this book, we're going to talk about the life of the famous military commander, Alexander the Great. So, let's get right to it!

View of Macedonian city Ohrid

MACEDON IN NORTHERN GREECE

Alexander was born in Macedon also called Macedonia, a country located in what is now the northern part of Greece. The name of the country came from the Mackednoi tribe who lived there.

The citizens of Macedon didn't have much communication with the people living in southern Greece and didn't get involved with the constant fighting between the city-states of southern Greece. Even after they were invaded by the Persians in 480 BC, the Macedonians kept their distance. However, things changed when King Philip II took over the country in 359 BC.

Illustration of King Philip II of Macedon

At the time that King Philip II took over, Macedonia's army was weak and unorganized. He strengthened the army and made them into a forceful group of professional soldiers.

After they were ready, Philip went forward to conquer the city-states to the south and they became part of Macedonia. Macedonia had become a powerful empire.

A village in Epirus, Greece

A PROPHETIC DREAM

During those days, kings frequently wed more than one wife. Sometimes they selected wives based on alliances they needed to make with other countries. King Philip took Olympias who came from the region of Epirus as his second wife.

The night before their wedding night, Olympias had a dream that a bolt of lightning hit her womb and that a raging fire came out of it. Philip had a dream that he was placing a seal with the figure of a lion on her womb. These dreams were interpreted to mean that their offspring was going to be a great leader.

Olympias Monument and fountain, Skopje, Macedonia

Statue of Alexander the Great

I n fact, legend told that the soon-to-be born child's father was actually Zeus, the Greek god of thunder and lightning. In 356 BC, Olympias had a son and she and Philip named him Alexander. When he reached the height of his military career, he would be known as Alexander the Great.

ALEXANDER'S EARLY LIFE

Alexander and his younger sister spent much of their time in the royal court. Their mother was a strong woman and she raised them because his father was almost always away on military campaigns. Even though his father was away, he wanted Alexander to get a good education so he hired tutors for him.

Olympias presenting the young Alexander the Great to Aristotle

Alexander and his tutor

Alexander's first tutor was a man named Leonidas. He taught the young boy mathematics as well as the sports of horsemanship and archery, which would be important to a future soldier. Alexander was an unruly student and soon King Philip had to hire another tutor.

The next tutor's name was Lysimachus. To keep Alexander engaged in his studies they would role play famous battles. Alexander loved these military strategy activities as he took on the role of Achilles, the famous Greek warrior.

Alexander and Lysimachus

Aristotle and Alexander

ARISTOTLE BECOMES ALEXANDER'S TUTOR

In 343 BC, King Philip hired Aristotle, the famous philosopher, to tutor his son. Aristotle introduced Alexander to the famous Greek poem the Iliad. This 15,000 line long poem is about the epic Trojan War. Alexander liked the poem so much that Aristotle wrote a summary version of it that Alexander could take with him.

At the age of sixteen, Alexander became a soldier in the Greek army. He fought side by side with his father in a critical battle against the Athenians and Thebans.

After King Philip was successful in unifying southern and northern Greece, things shifted. Philip took another wife by the name of Cleopatra Eurydice. This was the cause of great distress for Olympias.

Alexander became a soldier in the Greek army.

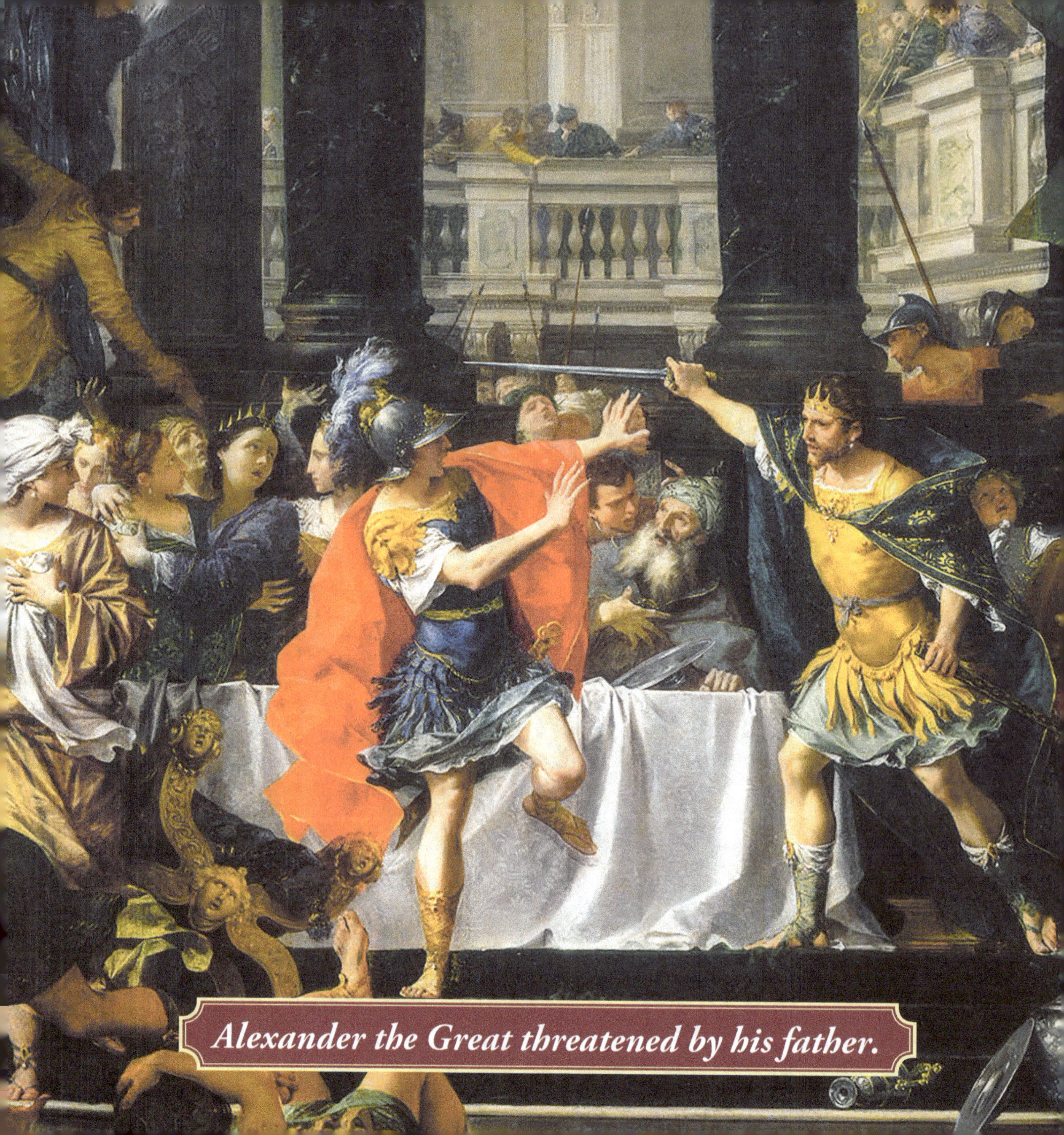

Alexander the Great threatened by his father.

The other problem was that there was tension between Philip and his son. Alexander had become intelligent and wise beyond his years. Perhaps Philip found his own son was now a threat to his throne. He banished Olympias, Alexander, and Alexander's sister.

ALEXANDER BECOMES KING OF MACEDONIA

Alexander's sister was getting married and King Philip was at the event. Normally the king would have had numerous bodyguards, but he asked them to leave him by himself for a while. However, one of the bodyguards stayed. He plunged a dagger into Philip and killed him. Many historians believe that Olympias and possibly even Alexander planned this murder, but no one knows for sure.

Assassination of King Philip of Macedon

Alexander gained the army's trust
so they would want him to be king.

He was only 19-years-old at the time, but Alexander knew what to do. He gained the army's trust so they would want him to be king. To make sure that her son would be king, Olympias had Philip's other children, a girl called Europa and a boy called Caranus, killed so they couldn't inherit the throne. When their mother Cleopatra Eurydice found out that they had been killed, she killed herself.

ALEXANDER'S MILITARY CONQUESTS

Alexander was now king and he acted swiftly. He gained the support of all the Greek city-states with the exception of Athens. He started making plans to take over the huge empire of Persia located to the east.

Alexander gained the support of all the Greek city-states with the exception of Athens.

Alexander led his enormous army of 3000 cavalry as well as 30,000 infantry to Thebes.

Before he could take action, he got word that Thebes, one of the Greek city-states had forced his troops out of the city. This could have caused a revolt of the once-united city-states so he led his enormous army of 3000 cavalry as well as 30,000 infantry to the southern region of the country's peninsula.

For their disloyalty, he destroyed the city of Thebes. The other city-states became fearful that they would be destroyed as well so they pledged their loyalty to him. Even Athens pledged their allegiance.

The sacking of Thebes by Alexander the Great

Alexander the Great discovering
the body of Darius King of Persia.

Now that the country was united again, it was time for new conquests. In 334 BC he defeated the Persian army over several battles. Once he had captured the Persian king, King Darius, he took over the country and proclaimed himself king.

Next, he wanted to conquer the civilization of Egypt. He quickly achieved that conquest and in 331 BC he established the cultural center of Alexandria, named for him. This city housed a great library and became an important commerce hub. Later that same year, he was victorious at the Battle of Gaugamela even though he and his troops were greatly outnumbered. He was now king of Babylon as well as Asia.

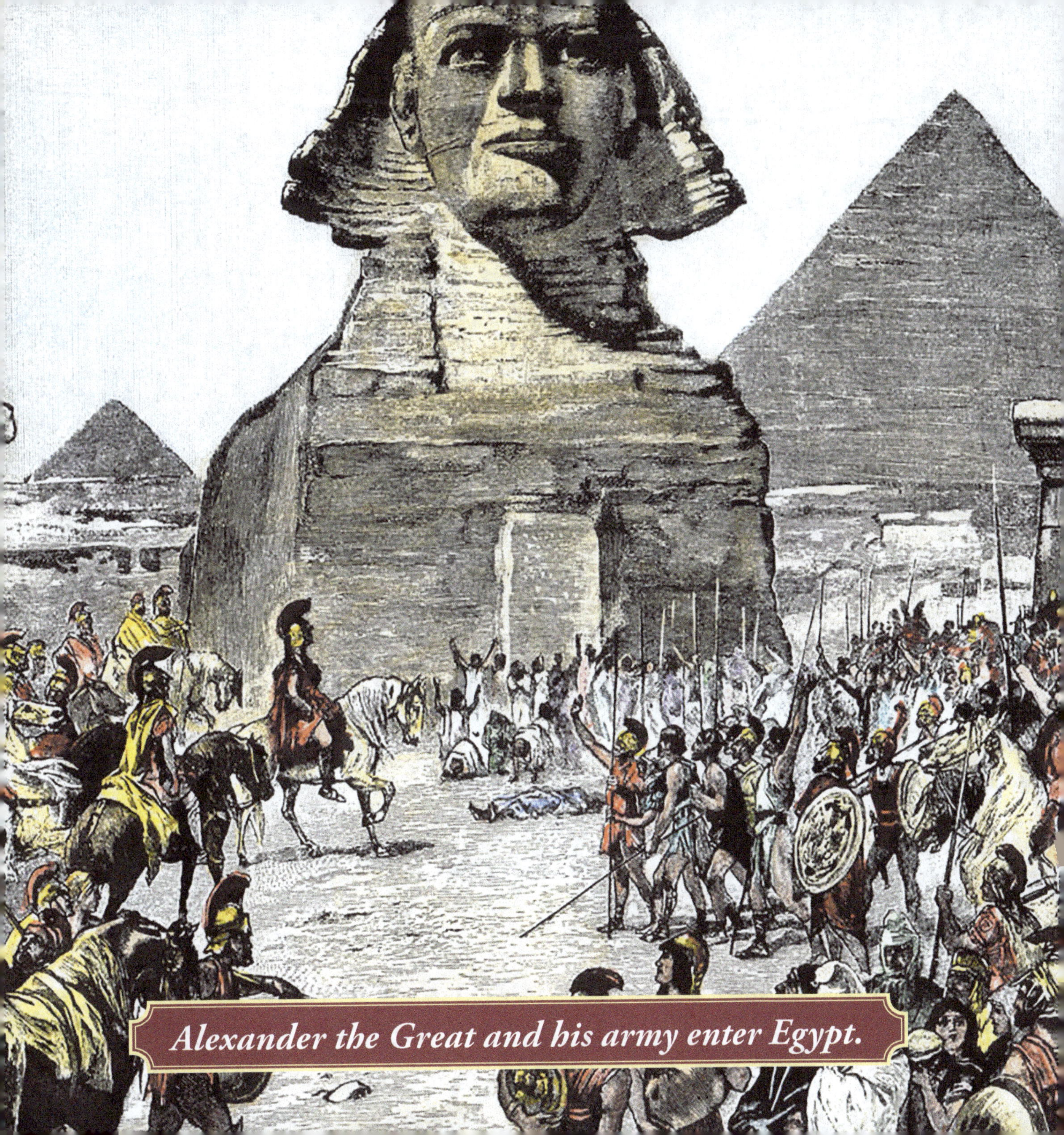

Alexander the Great and his army enter Egypt.

The marriage of Alexander the Great and Roxana

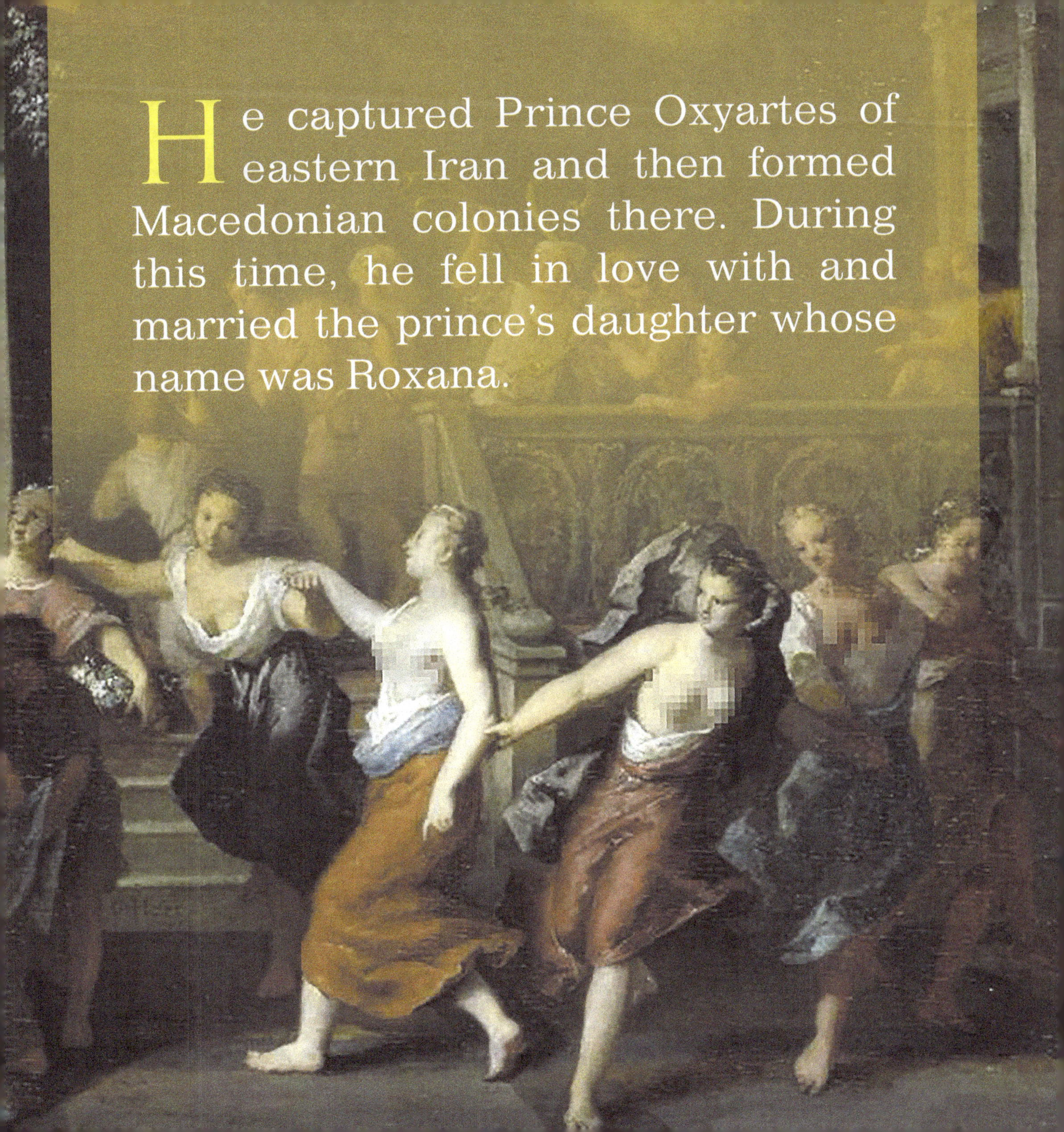
He captured Prince Oxyartes of eastern Iran and then formed Macedonian colonies there. During this time, he fell in love with and married the prince's daughter whose name was Roxana.

Alexander had decided to march on India next. After his armies were victorious there, he did something unusual. He was impressed with India's king and returned him to his throne, although India was now part of Alexander's growing empire and were no longer self-ruling.

King Porus of India surrenders to
Alexander the Great.

Alexander was wounded by an
enemy soldier, but he rebounded.

His troops were weary though. They wanted to go back to their families in Macedonia. On their return trip, Alexander was wounded by an enemy soldier, but he rebounded.

In 324 BC they arrived in Susa, now a city in Iran. As a strategic move to unify Persia with Macedonia, he dictated that Macedonians must marry Persian princesses. He also gained thousands of soldiers from Persia for his armies and sometimes dismissed Macedonians, which made those soldiers who were loyal to him very angry. He saw their unrest and killed some of the Persian leaders to appease them and regain their trust again.

Alexander the Great in the temple of Jerusalem

Soldiers paying final tribute to the dying Alexander the Great.

THE DEATH OF ALEXANDER

Alexander was thirty-two years old when he became very ill with a high fever and died within ten days. It wasn't clear if he had contracted malaria or if he'd been poisoned. A few months after he died, his wife had a baby boy. Unfortunately, Alexander's son never became king. He was killed by a rival for the throne when he was only 13 years old.

THE LEGACY OF ALEXANDER

Alexander the Great is regarded as the most accomplished military genius of ancient times. During his short life, he conquered lands from Greece all the way to Egypt. He had dominion over present-day Turkey as well as Pakistan and Iran.

Alexander the Great conquered lands from Greece all the way to Egypt.

Alexander at the tomb of Achilles

He was extremely successful in battle but he also worked toward promoting cultural exchanges among the countries now in his empire so they would blend together as one nation. The stories of his achievements grew and were told over and over. There was speculation that he had royal blood from the gods running through his veins.

ALEXANDER THE GREAT AND DIOGENES

Alexander's early education gave him a thirst for knowledge. During his lifetime, he would seek out famous philosophers and engage them in conversations. Legend has it that one day he went to see the famous philosopher, Diogenes. Diogenes was in the public square when Alexander found him.

Alexander visits Diogenes

Diogenes

Alexander was already a prince and he was powerful and wealthy. He asked Diogenes if there was anything he needed or anything he could offer to him. Diogenes replied, "Yes! You're blocking the sun. Please move aside." Alexander thought it was funny and was impressed by Diogenes' refusal to be awestruck in his presence. He said, "If I were not Alexander, I would be the philosopher Diogenes."

The entrance of Alexander the Great in Babylon

Awesome! Now you know more about the life and achievements of Alexander the Great. You can find more Biography books from Baby Professor by searching the website of your favorite book retailer.

Visit

BABY PROFESSOR
EDUCATION KIDS

www.BabyProfessorBooks.com
to download Free Baby Professor eBooks and view
our catalog of new and exciting Children's Books